Cleaning Tent Tops for Happier Customers and Better Profits

A Complete How-to Guide to Cleaning Party Rental Tents

By Steve Arendt

ISBN-13: 978-06922004-4-5
ISBN-10: 0692200444

Published by Teeco Solutions
www.TeecoSolutions.com
1-877-712-9172

Edited by Jennifer-Crystal Johnson
www.JenniferCrystalJohnson.com

Book Cover Design by Jennifer-Crystal Johnson
www.JenniferCrystalJohnson.com

About the Author

Steve Arendt has been thinking 'out of the box' for a while now and has always had an entrepreneurial spirit. A few years after starting and growing a successful St. Louis tent rental business from the ground up, Steve's desire to increase profits propelled him to taking a long, hard, realistic look at the industry as a whole. As part of the discovery process, he evaluated and examined systems and methods of the industry as well as productivity and accounting and found that, not only did he enjoy developing more efficient ways of doing things, he also enjoyed sharing this information and knowledge with others. As a result, he sold his tent rental business (The Tent Event) and founded Teeco Solutions in 2000.

As CEO of Teeco Solutions, Steve's experience, expertise, and energy are focused on better lives through better business by mechanizing the manual and offering viable and practical solutions to the challenges of the party tent rental industry. Steve holds a Bachelor's Degree in Communication & Marketing from St. Louis University and his professional affiliations include: Entrepreneur Organization, IFAI, ARA, and MATRA. Beyond business, Steve is an active volunteer and board member in his community, has been married for over 20 years, is the proud father of three sons, and makes his home in St. Louis, Missouri.

Acknowledgements

The road to becoming the leader in tent cleaning was very serendipitous and could not have been traveled without the help of many people around me. First and foremost is my wife of over 20 years, Becky. Without her support and encouragement, none of this would be possible. She has allowed me to grow as a business person, husband, and father. Our three boys have shown me that life is a balance between the great thrill of business and the softer side of life required to thrive in our world.

My first team at The Tent Event LLC was awesome. They supported me, they challenged me, and they grew with me. I owe much gratitude to all the men and women that helped grow our first company.

At key points in my life, it seems that just the right mentor or coach showed up to help me and teach me. As I look back, the list is long. Some have been with me for years and some only for short periods. A special thanks goes out to Fr. Jerry Meier for all his wisdom about everything throughout the years.

The folks at the Vistage organization have played key roles in our success. I would also especially like to acknowledge my EO forum group. Through the years, this group of business owners has served as my personal and business board of directors. Their insights, direction, and shared experiences have been indescribably invaluable.

A quick shout-out to my parents.... Throughout all of my childhood they modeled what it meant to be great businesspeople, business owners, and parents. Thank you for showing me that this could be done.

Finally, the team at Teeco Solutions, who are top notch people doing top notch things. The guys and gals in engineering, machining, and fabrication allow me to take any idea to final product in a way that is unmatched in the world. They are truly a gifted set of individuals who are indispensable to the organization. The people in our sales and marketing teams are incredible. These people are always learning, always challenging me, and always forcing me to grow. It is a true pleasure coming in to work each day to be with this team.

About Us

It was 1997 and we were just getting started. We had nothing but time, energy, a pick-up truck, a barn, and a desire to succeed. An idea germinated: a service-oriented tent rental business could work here. Time passed. A service-oriented tent rental business *did* work here. Three years later, we had a few employees, a few trucks, our business was growing, and sales were good; but not great. Between the long, taxing hours we were putting in and the money coming in – although decent – it didn't add up. Something had to change. What would it take to get from good to great, to move our business to the next level? After a long, hard look at every aspect of the business, we had an "aha" moment. We realized that *efficiency was the key and overall inefficiency was hindering growth.* Long story short, we strive to meet the needs of those who own and put up tents. Our goal is simple: we want to make party rental firms more efficient and more profitable.

We are no longer in the tent rental business. Now, we specialize in providing tent washing and drying machines to party tent rental businesses throughout the world. Teeco Solutions is the worldwide leading provider of machines to solve the issue of cleaning tents. Teeco Solutions has over 44,000 square feet of engineering, machining, and fabrication facilities. A full-time service staff, a full-time sales staff, a full-time marketing staff, a full-time engineering staff, and a full-time assembly staff are always working hard to make cleaning tents a much easier and more profitable proposition for companies like yours. This means that there are over 40 people available to serve you and solve the cleaning needs of your company.

If you have any questions or need to talk about tent cleaning, contact us:

www.TeecoSolutions.com
1-877-712-9172

Table of Contents

Steve Arendt

Introduction

Owning or operating a tent rental company is hard work. I know because I started one from scratch and built it into a profitable and thriving business. The journey was exciting, fun, and full of hidden roadblocks.

This book is written to help those who own or operate a tent rental company become better by examining the invisible barriers of something as simple as dirty tent tops and the effect they have on the profitability, efficiency, and overall wellbeing of a typical tent rental company.

Once my tent rental business was operating profitably and successfully, I started to study the amount of money I was getting paid per hour. The findings changed the course of my life. I was NOT getting paid very much for the amount of effort and time I was putting into the company. This epiphany caused a landslide of analysis to find out how to change my plight. What I found was that we were consistently doing certain things the hard way and the wrong way every time we did them. This is what Albert Einstein called insanity – doing the same thing over and over and expecting different results. I was working insanely hard for little money.

Further analysis revealed that the seemingly insignificant issue of cleaning tent tops was a major contributor to my insanity. If tops weren't clean, they quickly affected every area of my business: customers complained, employees' morale suffered, rewashing was costly, and never having enough tops to supply my high-end events was costly. The more I dug, the more was revealed. Getting tents as clean as possible, as quickly as possible, as often as possible, and in such a way that I would not have to worry was the first priority to solving my insanity.

We solved the problem and, since then, have gone on to solve this issue for countless companies across the world. My work has brought me across the globe and I have spoken to many trade organizations about my experiences and understanding on this topic. Through the years, countless people have encouraged me to write a book about my experience. They wanted me to share with any growing tent rental company the lessons I learned the hard way.

Recently, the opportunity presented itself. At first I was apprehensive. As the person responsible for the growth and prosperity of the company, I could not see how it would be possible to carve out the time to write about my experiences. With the help of others who are smarter than I am (it is always good to surround yourself with such people), I learned of a way to make it happen. Initially, I was encouraged to take a few days away for the purpose of recording my experiences as audio. With the help of an interviewer, I was able to organize my thoughts and record a concise and short account of the things I have learned along the way. Once we had it transcribed, I was able to more quickly refine and edit my thoughts. With the insights and help of my editor (thank you, Jennifer-Crystal Johnson), we decided to keep the interview style of the book.

My thought is that you, too, may be too busy growing a company to read this book in its entirety, but by browsing through the various questions posed, you can pick out the most important answers to what is currently keeping you from growing your business.

Chapter One

Three Basic Ways to Wash a Party Tent

The tent rental business is hard. My father told me that when I started my first tent rental business. Initially I ignored him, but a few years later I understood what he was talking about.

Because the business is seasonal, the management of cash flow requires a bit of discipline and knowledge. You have to be part accountant to successfully grow; there's lots of money when things are going strong and always less than desired when the season is slow. You have to be part human resources expert, too. How do you keep great people that you can only keep busy for part of the year?

As the business grows, so does the need to purchase more inventory. I've not yet met a tent rental operator that claimed to have as many tents as they need or the correct styles for their market; there always seems to be an appetite to get more tents. As the owner or operator, you also have to be part CFO to manage the inventory correctly. The need for more trucks, more building space, and more outside storage seems to be a never-ending demand on the cash that is available. My father did say that if I could master the growth of a tent rental company, I will have developed the skills to be a great business person. Once again, he was right. Running a tent rental business requires knowledge, skills, and successful execution in all areas of business. The person who can do it successfully is very talented.

This book is for those people who always want to learn more. It focuses on just one aspect of the business: the cleaning of tents. Yet, experience has shown us that the cleaning of tents goes way beyond the technical aspect of how to keep them clean. The issue of keeping tents clean affects all areas of your business.

The rest of this book is written in a format that reads like an interview, and is written for the busy tent rental owner or operator who desires to learn more, be challenged, and needs to do it on their own time. Take the time to read the entire book or find the questions that are important to you and read the answers.

What are the various cleaning processes available?

There are three basic cleaning processes available and you really have to dive into your own business, as we're going to find out in this book, to understand what's best for you.

You can spread out your tent on a floor and use mops, rags, brushes, or floor polishers to clean them. You could buy a machine and put that in your building to wash your tents, and you can also use a process utilizing tables, a spray and wash type of process, and we'll talk more about that a little later.

What are the advantages and disadvantages of washing by hand and can you tell us a little about how the hand washing processes works?

Oh, when you wash by hand, it can be inexpensive. It's good for a business with lots of extra space and you can build great systems to get your production level to where it needs to be.

The key area here is to really look at your wash systems and understand how much vinyl or PVC your company needs to clean each day or week and build systems to a achieve this goal. I'm going to talk a lot more about productivity later in the book. Once you understand how much vinyl or PVC your company needs to efficiently keep up with demand and most efficiently use your inventory, hand washing may or may not be a viable solution.

Some advantages of washing by hand are that it's very good where labor is plentiful and inexpensive. Some disadvantages of washing by hand are that production can be slow and quality control is in the hands of humans. Often, consistent quality control is not achievable without a great management process around it, and hiring a great management team can be costly for a business not large enough to support this cost.

Also keep in mind that when washing by hand it is nearly impossible to completely clean all the webbing, straps, and ropes attached to a tent top. Cleaning by hand is only good for keeping the PVC or vinyl clean.

The most common process of cleaning by hand is to simply lay a tent top on the floor and clean it as you might clean a floor. The most common tools used to clean tents on the floor are mops, brushes, rags, and floor polishers.

Many companies use a mop as the tool of choice for cleaning on the floor. Like mopping a floor, simply fill a bucket with water and cleaning solution and use the mop like you would on a floor. Before the cleaning solution is allowed to dry, make sure to thoroughly rinse off the top with a hose and clean water. <u>Leaving any residual cleaning solutions on the tent top has huge negative impacts on the tops months down the road.</u>

TIP – When you're using mops, you might want to go to the local roofing supply store and buy what they call a 24 or 36 ounce mop. It's a much heavier mop than you can find in regular places and that will really help you in terms of increasing your productivity.

Some companies use brushes instead of mops to clean tent tops on the floor. Brushes can offer one clear advantage over a mop: a deeper level of clean. However, there are drawbacks. When using a brush that is too stiff, the employees will see great cleaning results, but they will inadvertently be damaging the tent tops. A brush that is too stiff not only removes dirt, but it will remove and scratch the outer surfaces of the vinyl. This causes premature wear on the top and the newly scratched surface provides a great place to collect even more dirt on the next rental, forcing you to wash the top more often. The trick when using brushes is to find a brush that is stiff enough to clean yet soft enough not to damage the tent top.

TIP – Very often such a brush can be found at a retail pool supply store. Also pay attention to the type of brush that is used in a self-serve car wash; a brush similar to this style is often a great solution.

Most often the brush is mounted to a handle and dipped into a bucket of cleaning solution prior to scrubbing the tent tops. Rinsing takes place just as it does when using a mop.

Using rags to wash on the floor can offer a remarkable result. The results are most remarkable because the person who is doing the cleaning is forced to be on their knees. Their eyes are closer to the fabric, so they'll see more of the dirt and be inclined to do a better job of cleaning.

TIP – When using rags, make sure to use a terrycloth rag like a bath towel. Unlike a rag similar to a t-shirt, a terrycloth rag has small "bristles" that will reach into the imperfections of the vinyl where the dirt is hiding.

TIP – Later in the book we talk about the importance of using a smooth floor, and it is ultra-important if using rags to clean tent tops. Although the cleaning results can be very good, using a rag and washing on the floor is the most inefficient, costly, and slow way to wash a tent top. Employees do not prefer it and morale for those who wash this way is often very low.

The use of floor polishers is a tricky proposition. On one hand, the results are awesome. Yet if there is not a strict protocol and set of instructions that is followed each time, it's really easy to inflict serious damage on a tent top. When using a floor polisher, it is extremely important to use the least aggressive and most soft pad you can find.

TIP – When shopping for a pad, you have many options you can choose from, and enlisting the help of a local commercial janitorial supply company expert is often a wise choice.

TIP – I have witnessed employees take a brand new pad and wear it down (thus making it even softer) by putting the pad on the polisher and operating it directly on the rough surface of a sidewalk prior to using the pad on a tent top. It seems that quickly operating the polisher on the roughness of the sidewalk can change the nature of the pad to become softer.

The biggest advantage of using a floor polisher is that the polishing machine does all of the actual work of scrubbing. The employee does not have to provide the effort needed to clean the tent. Additionally, the design of the pad will act like the terrycloth rag we talked about earlier. Dirt finds its way into the imperfections of the PVC or vinyl, and having a pad that can reach into these imperfections to clean the dirt is key.

TIP – When discovering how to use a floor polisher for the first time or when training a new employee, always use a tent top that you can afford to destroy. Mastering the technique of using a floor polisher often means that the operator does not move the polisher at a quick enough pace and can easily "burn through" the outer layers of PVC or vinyl. Before a new employee uses a polisher on a nice top, make sure that they are properly trained.

Very often, cleaning chemicals are mixed into a portable pressurized sprayer and sprayed onto the top prior to using the floor polisher. It's really important to ensure that the floor polisher is not used on a dry tent top. Some systems even advocate applying a large volume of water and cleaning solution to the top prior to using the polisher to ensure the correct amount of liquid between the polishing pad and the tent top. It's better to err on the side of caution by using too much liquid rather than not enough. When done cleaning, make sure to rinse the top thoroughly with clean water.

TIP – When washing tent tops on the floor, make sure that all gravel and pebbles are removed from the floor prior to spreading the top out for cleaning. If a pebble or a rock is not removed, the pressure of a foot walking over, a brush, a mop, or a rag will cause a pinhole to form in the tent top. Additionally, make sure the floor is completely clean. Most tent rental companies will pressure wash the floor prior to laying tent tops out for cleaning.

When washing by hand, the selection of cleaning chemicals is very important. Buying the wrong chemicals can cause premature wear on your tent tops and can cause you to spend more on labor to get the tops clean. We're going to talk a little bit about chemicals later in the book. To try some safe cleaning agents for your cleaning operation, take advantage of the special offer at www.teecosolutions.com/samplepak.

Why and when is it best to use a tent washing machine?

Tent washing machines are not for everybody. But you would want to take a look at using a tent washing machine during times in your business when you have too much daily volume to keep up with through the use of a hand cleaning method. So in other words, you have a dirty pile there that is really starting to inhibit your business on a day to day basis, especially when you're busy.

Other times in your business when you want to start looking and perhaps getting involved in machine washing your tent tops is when your A-grade tops don't last five to seven years. Tent washing machines offer the deepest cleaning possible and extend the lifespan of a tent top in A-grade condition. If your A-grade tops are lasting you anywhere between two, three, or four years, you're really not getting the full potential of an A-grade top.

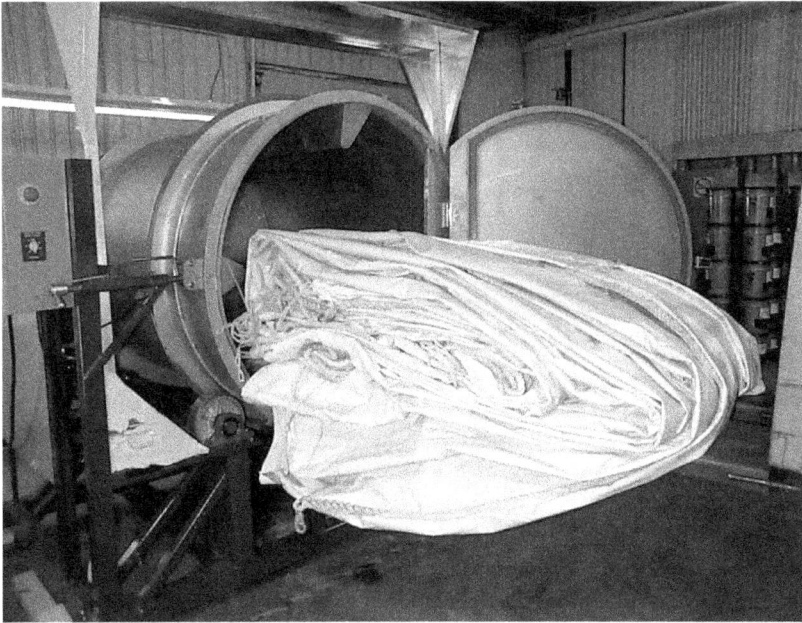

When you have a clean, pristine A-grade top and you rent it, you can charge more money for it. Many owners and operators get too busy with growing their companies to realize the implications of charging more money. In the sense of having an A-grade top, one may or may not charge more for the actual tent. But think about this – usually an A-grade tent is going to be set up at a wedding or a nicer event. It is these events that require the most profitable items in your inventory: your accessories!

Think about it this way. Even if you do not charge any more for an A-grade tent compared to a B- or C-grade tent, it still takes the same amount of manpower to put it up, so your cost and profit are exactly the same for setting up a tent. But the real gain is being able to use the same labor force to install the accessories like lighting, sidewall, tent liners, tables, chairs, flooring, etc. Even if you don't choose to charge more for a clean tent, it is a great tool to get the jobs that require your most profitable items in your inventory.

So, the longer that you can maintain that top as a pristine grade, usually about five to seven years, the more money you're actually going to get out of that investment in your top. It's a good time to start looking at tent washing machines when you can't get a long-term A-grade level out of a particular top using the system that you're using. To learn more about tent washing machines visit www.TeecoSolutions.com.

Another time when you want to use or consider washing in a machine is when you can no longer control the quality of clean that your company produces. This usually happens when a company is growing. So initially, when you start your company, you'll be able to have good quality control over the process of cleaning. As you grow, you start cycling employees through that don't know what they're doing, and you are too busy to stop and train them. Often what happens is the process that you have in place starts to change unbeknownst to you; a lot of times your quality control will change and your quality of clean tends to go down.

DID YOU KNOW? There are basically two different designs for tent washing machines: machines that tumble and clean any style tops and machines designed to wash and dry only the flat panels found in structure tents. To learn more about the differences and capabilities of these, visit:

www.teecosolutions.com/tumbler-flat-panel-comparison

Sometimes you don't become aware of this until customers start complaining, and that can be a very bad thing for your business. So, if you want to gain quality control over consistently having a clean product, that's when tent washing machines can come into play.

The other reason you would want to look at getting a tent washing machine is when you're out of space. You can take up a 10 x 10 or 11 x 11 foot space, put a machine in there, and actually end up saving space in your business. We have even seen many operators put a tent washer outside.

TIP – *Using a tent washing machine is the only method of washing that can use the additional power of warm water to clean. Using a tent washer allows for a more effective combination of cleaning agents and provides the most foolproof way to guarantee that harmful chemical residues are not left on a tent top. The use of a tent washing machine will provide the most effective level of clean available.*

Are there any other ways to wash?

Yes. One of the most interesting ways I've ever seen to wash – and very, very few people that I've seen across the country and across the world use it – is a system utilizing tables. I learned this from a person who had very little space in their building. Washing by hand made a lot of sense for them, but they had no place to dry the tents.

What they did was set a series of eight-foot tables up end to end. They were the 30-inch wide tables and they went three tables long, so it was 24 feet wide when they were washing their 20-foot wide tent tops. They actually lifted the fabric up on the table and used a very powerful and safe cleaner; they sprayed it on and then used a terrycloth rag to wipe way the dirt. It's really important to know that when you're washing tents with a rag to use terrycloth rags. So they would spray it on, let it sit for a little bit, and then wipe it off. They used such a powerful cleaner that it got even the deepest grime off.

TIP – A powerful and safe cleaning agent is imperative to have when using this method. Finding the correct cleaning agent for your dirt will take some homework. Visit www.teecosolutions.com/samplepak for a special deal on some great cleaning agents.

But there is an even bigger advantage to using this method. When they got done wiping it, they didn't have to dry that tent. It was a little more labor intensive up front, but they skipped the whole drying process. A little bit slower in the production, but it worked really well when space was tight and they weren't in a position to get a tent washing machine.

So, what's the right thing for me?

That's a great question. It's really, really important to understand that not every process is right for you.

But, to understand what's right for you, you really have to stop, think, and analyze your business. You have to start asking yourself:

- What is the number of tops that I have to wash at any one given time?
- What is the number of tent tops that I have to get washed during my slow time?
- What is the number of tent tops that I have to get washed during my busiest time?
- When my tops are returned, do I get my tops ready to re-rent quickly enough so that I always have the amount of tops I need even in my busiest times?

- What kind of space do I have available to wash tents during my busiest time?
- What kind of space do I have available to wash tents in the winter time?
- Do I always have a skilled and enthusiastic set of employees available to clean tents?
- What are my management costs associated with keeping tent tops clean?
- Am I often worried that a customer may complain about how dirty my tops are? Does this worry affect me as the leader of the company?

When you stop, think, and analyze it, the answer to what process is good for you is going to become very clear only after you have understood what your current production rates are, what production rates are actually needed in your company, and the other implications when you answer these questions.

You're going to have to understand by using your numbers and looking back at your sales what your yearly laundry volumes are. Your laundry loads per year are different than your actual inventory because you wash your inventory multiple times a year. So, what is the square footage of laundry that you complete in a given year? Or maybe, more importantly, what do you still have to complete? Maybe not what you did complete, but ideally what you *want* to complete. Gaining an accurate picture of what your annual laundry needs are will help you to decide what washing process is right for you.

TIP – When calculating your annual laundry loads, do not forget about your sidewall. There are many reasons that sidewall gets dirtier than tent tops, yet it is the most important piece of vinyl to keep clean. It is the piece that is closest to the customers' eyes! When we help companies calculate their actual laundry needs when cleaning tents, we often find that sidewall cleaning accounts for 30% to 40% of their total laundry!

You also have to ask yourself what level of clean you really need. What are your customers' expectations? Not all people do weddings and high-end events, so you may not need a level of clean appropriate for those. After you really stop and think about it, ask your customers and ask your employees; that can really play into what kind of systems you have for your business.

To make sure you're really considering everything, you also have to ask yourself:

- Am I buying new tops just to keep a large inventory of A-grade stuff available as the rest of them deteriorate and get dirty over time?
- Am I buying new tops at the same rate I've always bought them because I've got a great cleaning process in place and am just always adding to my A-grade inventory?
- Am I fully utilizing every top I own to accommodate my growing company?

Steve Arendt

Chapter Two

Common Pitfalls to Avoid When Cleaning a Tent

What are the common pitfalls to avoid?

I've been all over the world and there are lots of common pitfalls to avoid. The first has to do with chemicals. The second has to do with rinsing. And the third thing we'll talk about is tools.

Having the wrong chemicals or not allowing the chemicals to do their job is very, very important. We'll also talk about rinsing and the long-term effects of not rinsing as *the* most common thing I see overlooked in any washing process.

Often when we talk about tools, people just go to the local hardware or janitorial supply store and buy whatever is on the shelf. They don't pay attention to getting the right tools; maybe they go to the local hardware store and buy whatever looks good as they are standing at the shelf. They don't take the time beforehand to understand and learn exactly what they need. There's a fourth area about pitfalls to avoid, and that's not getting the tent tops professionally cleaned at least once or twice a year. This can really help in getting your A-grade tops not to fall to the B-grade level so fast.

How do you avoid misusing chemicals?

This is a great question that most people overlook. When you select the wrong chemicals, it can increase your labor cost. If you have a chemical that's not very effective at cleaning the actual dirt, your people are going to have to scrub longer. And when they're scrubbing longer, they can't do as well as they really want to do, so you've given them a chemical that's not really suited to get the tent top clean at the level that you want. So they're not only going to scrub longer, but their morale is going to go down and they're not going to scrub long and hard for *you*, and so, the cost of labor is going to go up.

If you select the wrong chemical, it can also damage the tent top. A lot of times I see clients who go to the local store and just buy whatever chemical is on the shelf, and that will have long-term effects on the stitching, it will have long-term effects on the PVC, and it will deteriorate it very prematurely, so they need to spend some time and think about the right chemical.

TIP – A quick and easy test to see if a chemical will harm a tent top is to find a clean black or dark blue rag. Apply the cleaning solution to the rag in liberal amounts. Then start rubbing the rag on a clean piece of white PVC or vinyl. Inspect the rag. If the rag picks up the white from the vinyl, it means that the cleaning solutions you are choosing are dissolving or deteriorating the tent fabric. Note: even if there is no residue on the rag, further investigation as to the safety of the cleaning agent may be required.

I would also avoid the temptation to start washing too quickly. This is a really, really big point. Too often, in the name of production, we want to apply the chemical to the surface and just start scrubbing right away. Your best method is to go ahead and apply the chemical to the surface and allow it to sit there for a time. Very often on the label it will give you suggested amounts of time called dwell times. That chemical needs time to react with the dirt and lift it off of the surface, and that, in essence, is doing a lot of the work for us.

If you start scrubbing on the surface a little bit too prematurely, you're doing more work than you need to. Over time it's actually going to slow your production down and increase your labor cost. So, avoid the temptation to start washing too quickly. Get the chemical on there and allow it to sit for a little bit.

What about using bleach as part of the process for cleaning tents?

This is probably the most common question that I get about tent washing. Bleach may be one of the best cleaning agents around. However, it also has some very negative side effects.

Tent rental operators are most tempted to use bleach when they discover that their tops have been attacked by mold. Perhaps there is no better solution for removal of mold than bleach; however, there are some things you must know.

First off, bleach is not recommended for use with vinyl. I would highly recommend you do the following test on your desk or bench to understand why.

Fill a disposable cup up with straight 6% bleach, fill a second cup up with half bleach and half water, fill a third up with 33% bleach and 66% water, a fourth at 10% bleach and 90% water, and a final one with 2% bleach and 98% water. Put a 1" x 1" sample of PVC/vinyl into each cup. After one minute, take note of the condition of each. Do the same for every minute up to 15 or 30 minutes. What you will see is that the one immersed in straight bleach will turn yellow and become brittle in only a few minutes, and the ones in the more diluted solutions will take longer to achieve this negative result.

The yellowing and brittleness is a result of removing what is referred to as the plasticizers. Plasticizers are used to keep the PVC/vinyl flexible. Bleach is also a cause of destruction to your tent top long after you have used it to clean the top. I often get calls about what I call "stitch rot." Stitch rot happens when the stitching that is used to sew webbing, straps, or ropes to a tent top suddenly fails and literally allows the strapping, webbing, or rope to be easily pulled away from the PVC or vinyl. Unfortunately, this happens most often on a busy tent rental day when a tent is being set up. Most don't realize that this is most often caused by the use of bleach a few months earlier. What happened was that bleach was used to clean a top and, most importantly, it was not completely rinsed off from the entire top. Even trace amounts of bleach left in the thread or stitching can cause failure over time.

Sometimes a tent renal operator is forced to use bleach in a cleaning process, especially when the alternative is to throw a tent top in the trash unless it comes clean. In this case, special care and processes must be followed and the most important aspect is to ensure that the time the vinyl has been exposed to the bleach is minimal, that the concentration of bleach used was not too much, and that ALL traces of bleach were rinsed from the entire top (including all webbing, stitching, and ropes). When using a hand washing process to rinse tops, it is nearly impossible to guarantee that all of the bleach has been rinsed away. The only process that can offer an operator a guarantee that all bleach is rinsed is to use a tent washing machine.

CAUTION: When using a tent washing machine or contracting with a company that uses tent washing machines, ask to see their machine and ask them to show you how the rinsing operations work. If a tent washing machine has been designed to recycle 100% of the water used, be very cautious about how well your tents are being rinsed. For a list of tent cleaning contractors around you, go to www.teecosolutions.com/tent-washing-services.

TIP – Not all bleach you buy is the same. Most bleach sold in the supermarket or at the local retailer is a 6% solution. However if you buy bleach from a commercial or industrial supplier, you might be buying bleach that is twice as strong at 12%. If you are forced to use bleach, it pays to read the label to know what you're using.

CAUTION: Bleach can be harmful to vinyl PVC and all tent components. Never pour straight bleach onto a tent top, and if you are willing to take a risk by using bleach to extract a stain, consider diluting the bleach with water in a bucket prior to applying the mixture to the tent top.

Why is rinsing so important?

I call this the cardinal sin that I see time and time again across all processes. I know I just talked about this when we talked about the use of bleach, but it is worth repeating. Whether you're washing with mops, brushes, floor polishers, or machines, rinsing is extremely important. We often buy chemicals that are great for getting the dirt off, but they have a negative effect and it comes out in the stitching. The most common way we see this in the tent rental world is when we put a tent up and go to tighten and cinch it down; the strapping on it will tend to come loose. The stitching that stitches the strapping to the top just rots; we call it stitch rot. And you'll see it just tear that tent right down the line, just like the hem on your pants; it rips right up.

And that's really caused because some time earlier in the process of washing, the chemical was left in that stitching and it didn't get rinsed out. By then it's had a long time to start deteriorating and causing failure in the stitching, so not getting the rinsing done correctly can actually ruin your tent.

BIG TIP – When selecting the cleaning chemical that is right for your type of dirt, also test to make sure the chemical can be rinsed away easily. Not all chemicals have the same rinsing abilities.

Also, not getting the tent top rinsed has a very long-term effect because of the sun. The sun has UV rays and those UV rays will actually react with the residual chemical that's sitting on the

PVC. That will cause yellowing, and it will also cause brittleness and delamination. That's more of a long-term effect, but it definitely limits and shortens the life of the tent.

Why is using the wrong tools a costly mistake?

I mentioned earlier that often a client will go to the hardware store or the janitorial supply store and buy whatever is on the shelf or quickest to get and they will go to work. But if you use too stiff of a brush or a polishing pad for your floor polisher that's got too stiff of a property to it, it actually tears the top.

So it's important to understand how tops are made; they're made with a product called vinyl or PVC, and it's actually a fairly delicate product. If you go across that with a stiff brush or too stiff of a polishing pad, you're going to create abrasions in that surface. Dirt and mold spores can get into that area and start growing, and it's going to allow that dirt and mold to stay in these little microscopic scratches and make it harder to clean later on. It will also start to prematurely wear that top.

So, if you actually scratch a little bit too deep by using too stiff a brush or too stiff a polishing pad, you can promote what they call scrum mildew. Scrum mildew is when the actual PVC separates. Most tents in the USA are built in a layered system; the fabric itself is layered, so when those layers separate, water can get in between those layers kind of like getting in between the two pieces of bread on a sandwich where the meat is normally. Think of the scrum as being located where the meat on a sandwich is located. The scrum is sealed from both sides by two pieces of vinyl or PVC. Once water makes its way through the vinyl or PVC and into the scrum, the water will sit in there and it won't dry out because it's got no way to come out, and that's a perfect place for mold to grow. Once mold starts growing in between those layers, it's just a matter of time before a failure happens in that particular section of the tent.

NOTE – *Not all tent material is manufactured in a layered fashion (most often referred to as a laminate tent top). A more costly, rugged, and slightly heavier material is referred to as a coated material and has a tendency not to be affected by scrum mildew.*

So, using the wrong tool is a costly mistake when you also use a power washer. Oftentimes that's the first tool that people buy when they start the process of creating a system for their tents. But if you buy a power washer that only washes in cold, you're not able to take advantage of using warm or hot water in your cleaning process.

So buying a pressure washer that utilizes warm or hot water can be an advantage, but it can also be a disadvantage. If your water is too hot, what you're going to find is that you actually start to ever-so-slightly *melt* the surface of that vinyl and it's going to cause the surface of the tent to start deteriorating a little bit too quickly.

A very, very common damage from the power wash is when the user will actually take the pressure coming out of the wand of the power washer and get it too close to the tent. They will actually physically cut the tent or dig into a layer of the PVC and that causes it to deteriorate prematurely as well as causing all the things we talked about earlier – scrum mildew, tearing up the top, and microscopic tears.

Why is it best to get tent tops professionally cleaned?

I would highly recommend reaching out to somebody in your region who does tent top cleaning professionally at least once or twice a year, primarily because it makes for the best utilization of your tent tops that you can have. We talked earlier about the ability to maintain an A-grade top or a top that some people call wedding grade. Having your tent tops cleaned in a tent washing machine will provide you with the deepest level of clean you can get.

TIP – Go to www.teecosolutions.com/tent-washing-services to find a professional tent washing company hear you. These companies have machines specifically designed to wash and completely rinse tent tops. You did read about the importance of rinsing, right? If you can have a big inventory of wedding grade tops or A-grade tops, you can actually charge more for those tops every time they go out.

It's also important to understand that when you send tops out that are clean all the time, many things happen. First you have to understand that whether you're setting up a dirty tent or a clean tent, all the costs are the same. You still have to travel to get there, send the same crews out, and it takes the same amount of time to set them up.

But if you're setting up a tent that's clean, you can actually charge more for it. If you charge more for it, you have the same cost that you would having the same tent put up dirty, but you can actually have more profit for yourself. So you get more money in, your costs are the same, but you have more profit left for your own pocket as the owner or manager.

Also important to understand is that, by consistently putting up clean tops, you improve customer satisfaction. And when you improve customer satisfaction, it's a great, free way for your marketing and advertising to happen. It's called customer referrals. This is the best advertising that you can possibly have in this industry. When the party happens and all the people who are there look up and are very comfortable about the cleanliness of the product, they in turn call you for their next party.

It's very, very important to have customer satisfaction because the reverse can also happen. When you have customer dissatisfaction, those customers will tell ten of their friends – very quickly, in fact, more quickly compared to when they're satisfied – about how bad you are. Then you have to work double overtime to repair the damage that's done and spend a lot more money in advertising. So, it's important to at least have your tent tops professionally cleaned once or twice a year to get that deeper level of clean.

Chapter Three

Increasing Your Clean Tent Inventory by 10 to 20 Percent

What are some tips and tricks you can easily do to increase your clean top inventory?

The very first thing you can do is know the right chemicals to use. I have already talked about some aspects of cleaning chemicals, but what needs to be addressed is understanding your dirt.

When I attend tent conferences, people are always asking about the best cleaning agent to get tent tops clean. But often there's not a standard answer I can give them. This has to do with the type of dirt and stains that are common to each geographic region throughout the world. You must keep in mind that the dirt that makes tops dirty in Brisbane, Australia is not the same as the dirt in Boston, Massachusetts or Los Angeles, California. Furthermore, because the dirt is different, it means that a different cleaning agent may have to be used. So, not everyone throughout the world will use the same cleaning agents to keep their tops clean.

This means that you have to take the time to do some homework. You have to buy a number of cleaning agents and experiment to find what chemicals are safe and work best for your type of dirt. I often talk about doing this experiment during the slow times of the year.

If you take the time (it can take an entire day) to experiment with various cleaning chemicals, you can save yourself a great deal of money over time. Think about it this way: if you took eight hours of your day and found a chemical that would reduce the amount of human scrubbing required to clean your tops by a mere 15%, this means that your entire cleaning operation from that day forward would be improved by 10% to 15% and your employees would be that much happier because they would not have to scrub as hard and would have a new chemical that actually allowed them to get your tents as clean as you want them to be. You're setting your employees up for success and saving yourself a lot of money for a measly eight-hour one-time investment of your time!

OPPORTUNITY – Go to www.teecosolutions.com/samplepak for a special buy on your first three cleaning agents to try in your experiment. These are cleaning agents designed specifically for tent cleaning and offered to you especially because you took the time to read this book.

TIP – *Leaf stains and crepe paper. When you have stains left by crepe paper, leaves, or wet leaves rolled up and stored for a while on a top, you might want to use a strong toilet bowl cleaner. The one that I've often used is a brand called Sno Bowl and you can usually buy that in a hardware store. If that does not work, I have had reports that using an ultraviolent light left on to sit overnight can often lighten the stain. Finally, if none of these tricks work for your stain, then your only option is to paint over it. There is a special kind of paint or "ink" called vinyl ink. It was originally designed for hand painting vinyl signs. The ink comes in a variety of colors and can be found online or occasionally at an art supply store. Typically it is very thick in nature and can be applied with a brush. If you decide to thin the ink, I recommend using the thinning agent sold with it. I have had great luck with color matches and the ink's ability to adhere to the vinyl even through washing. The brand I have used with the most luck is Nazdar. Just google "Nazdar vinyl ink" to find out more.*

When you have stains that are tape, tar, or sticky, I would avoid using any solvent or citrus cleaners that can eat through the top. There's a really simple test you can do to test that tent cleaning chemical. You can take a black rag, put that chemical on it, and actually rub it onto the clean part of the tent. If you take that black rag off and it's got any white on it, you'll know that it's eating into the vinyl or the PVC of that tent top, so I wouldn't use that chemical. If you want a chemical that's really safe and highly effective, go to www.TeecoSolutions.com and take a look at buying our Tent Stain Eliminator. It is truly the best product on the market for this application.

The last thing you can do is to use a tent washing machine. When you use a tent washing machine, you are guaranteed 100% rinsing like we talked about earlier, so you won't have any stitch rot and you won't have any deterioration. Also, you're able to safely use warm or hot water in your washing process because warm and hot water greatly enhance the cleaning process.

You'll also find that, by using a tent washing machine, all the webbing can come clean. It's also a lot quicker than hand washing, and very often, you'll actually save space.

Can you share some more tips about how to experiment with chemicals so I can find the right chemicals to use?

It's really important to understand that the dirt that you have in your area is different than the dirt other people have in different areas of the county. We talked about experimenting. I want you to take the time to experiment with about seven to ten different types of chemicals. Make sure that you have the same level of dirt on your vinyl or PVC in your experimentation.

So, if you've got an extremely dirty tent that you really don't want to use or a piece of a tent that's dirty that you can cut up, cut it into little swatches to use as experiments because it's important that you have the same type of dirt as you go through this experiment.

When you use a specific chemical, I want you to experiment with at least three different dilution ratios as you go. Use the same brush on each experiment, but make sure that you rinse the brush each time you do a different test. Once you have used the same brush on the same dirty tent top with a good number of different cleaning chemicals and dilution ratios, simply ask your coworkers to rate which ones were the cleanest and find your winner.

When you do this experiment, you're also going to improve the quality of your clean. So what you're doing here is setting up a system that you're going to use in your busy time to ensure that your quality of clean is going to be consistent. This is a very important experiment.

When it comes to your busy time, you'll know for sure that you have the right chemical that's not destroying your tops or harming your employees.

Why does it make a difference what type of floor I scrub the tent on?

It makes a huge difference. Oddly enough, I didn't discover this until years into studying the cleaning processes, but a totally smooth floor is by far the best floor to scrub on. Often you've got a concrete floor that has a brushed finish to it. You most often see this on a sidewalk. Or you're going to go out and wash this on an asphalt surface that's not completely smooth. When I say smooth, I'm talking like a countertop that you might have in your kitchen. That's the level of smooth best used when washing tents.

When you use a smooth surface or a smooth floor to wash on, it actually reduces your scrubbing action, the amount of manpower, and your labor cost by 15% to 20%. It will also offer you a deeper level of clean and will increase your production.

Why might it make sense to use a tent washing machine?

Tent washing machines are used because you can get 100% of the washing and rinsing done and get it done every time. It's a system that the business owner or manager can have in place that can quickly teach even the lowest level of employee or a new employee to wash tents and expect the results to be 100%. Washing in a tent washer takes the element of human error out of the equation. You can use the tent washing machine as a way to leverage the warm water in your washing and get that deeper level of clean. The warm water reacts with the chemical and allows that chemical to act at its optimal level and really get in and wash all the strapping and the gray build-up that happens over time on the vinyl completely away.

You get all your webbing 100% clean because you've got a way not only for the chemicals to work and lift that dirt off, but also to go back and rinse that dirt away and send it down the drain. You can't really get it to that level of clean when you hand wash.

And lastly, when you use a tent washing machine you become a lot more productive, a lot more reliable, and a lot more controllable than any hand washing method. So, as your company grows, productivity, reliability, control, and systems have to start being put into place for effective, productive, profitable growth to happen, and that's when tent washing machines become really effective.

Steve Arendt

Chapter Four

Clearing the Clutter Without Expanding Your Building

How can I maximize my space and get my wash done without expanding my building?

Building space is premium in the tent rental world. When we talk about various areas of the tent rental business, space often becomes an issue because we tend to need a lot of space to operate this business. So, when we take a look at washing, often it's perceived as one of the systems that take up the most space, but it doesn't necessarily have to be that way.

I invite you start looking at your laundry volumes to determine exactly what amount of space you need and how much washing you are actually doing. Taking a look at those numbers will not only allow you to work your business more efficiently, but it will also let you grow and expand more easily.

Why is it so important to stop, think, and study my laundry volumes?

Very often I hear people talk about their washing process in terms of the actual inventory that they have, and those aren't the right numbers to look at. You have to look at the actual laundry volume because you have to understand that your inventory gets washed multiple times a year and these laundry volume numbers are unique to *your* business. You may want your inventory washed every time, you may want it washed once a year, twice a year, or four times a year.

Whatever your number is, how often you wash that inventory, you have to understand that it's a certain amount of square footage that you actually wash over a given year, and that's the number you have to focus on when you are looking at improving your business.

So, why is it so important that you stop, study, and look at the laundry volumes? It's important because you want to become a much more effective and productive business. You want to build a system within that business that allows the same amount of production per hour to happen every time the washing process takes place, so studying your laundry volume is a great place to start.

For example, when you start studying this, you will probably find that side walls make up 30-40% of your laundry volume. When you start to understand that little fact alone, you're going to build a different system to deal with your side walls so that you can get them out a lot quicker. They're smaller pieces, so there are certain things you can do within your process to make that go a lot faster. By looking at your laundry volume numbers, you are going to start to understand better ways to do it.

Why should you define peak laundry days?

We talked about defining your laundry volumes and you will tend to analyze your laundry volume annually. In order to do this, you can go back to your sales numbers and understand what tents went out and then calculate the total square footage you rented over the course of the year. By then dividing the amount of square footage rented annually by the average number of times you wash each piece, you can figure out your total laundry volume over a given year. But this alone is not enough. The next thing has to do with defining your peak laundry days.

Understanding that you have more laundry during your busy time than your non-busy time is key because, when you start building your system of cleaning around this, you have to build it with those particular days and weeks in mind – the times that are your busiest.

When you know exactly what to expect, this allows for better planning. So when you're in your busy time and you know that you're going to have a lot of laundry coming back in the upcoming weeks, you'll know how to better plan for it because you'll also know that you've got a system in place that is able to deal with this upcoming laundry load and you'll know exactly what that load is going to look like.

Ideally the plan would be to eliminate the dirty pile. By doing this you would be able to have dirty tops returned, processed, and back to the shelf ready to rent within 24 hours. Setting a goal similar to this is by far the most efficient use of the money you have invested in your tent top inventory.

KEY POINT – *Tent tops that sit in dirty piles or on shelves do not make you money! The only tent tops that make you money are the clean ones set up at a customer's site.*

How can I possibly get all this done in such a small space?

The very first thing you have to be is open-minded. If you tell yourself it can't be done in a small space, it won't get done; but

I can tell you that if you have a mindset that tells you that it *can* be done, you can figure it out. I've been all over the world and I have seen very, very unique ways of using small spaces.

And when I dive in to ask these owners and managers how they came up with the system for using this small space to get the laundry volumes that they need done in their business, they *always* tell me that they've asked their employees to work with them to come up with a creative plan to make that happen. They enter into a collaborative moment. Very often as a tent rental business owner or tent rental business manager, it's hard to include the employees. But these people have a wealth of knowledge because they do it day in and day out, and as the business owner or business manager, it's not something that you do. They bring a lot to the table, so allow them to help you. Set your goal with them and say, hey, we need to get X amount of production out of this space; how can we do this?

And the best time to go through this process is in your slow time. They really like to work with you and you'll improve their morale because they have some ownership involvement in that. It's key to be open-minded here and to include your employees in coming up with this process of using a small space and getting maximum production out of it.

The other key area is to tour other tent rental facilities across the country. If you don't have a good relationship with your competitor, go to the next county over and keep going out. As a rule, folks in our industry are very helpful to each other. And you're not alone; there are other people out there faced with the same problem, so reach out to your industry associations or vendors to help make introductions to people who have buildings and issues just like you; take the time to travel to them and ask them for half a day or a day of their time. Most people are extremely helpful and open to helping in these areas.

Can I save space by automating the cleaning process?

Absolutely. Most people feel that when they buy a washing machine or automate their washing process that it's actually going to take the same or more space. But when you automate your washing process, you also have to have an open mind and completely change the way you look at your washing system.

Because you can get a lot more laundry done in a quicker fashion by automating, you can actually use less space. You will also see opportunities that you never saw before.

One of the big opportunities that you're going to have available to you is that you can actually add a second shift, bringing two employees in after everybody else has gone. They work into the evening and are actually using space that's unavailable to them during the day when the trucks are coming and things are being loaded and unloaded. You can use that same space and use an automatic process or a washing machine to get the production that you need done so that when the daily crews come back in the morning, they can use the space that they normally use and have a pile of clean tents at the end. That can only be done when you have an automatic process that can wash very quickly.

By using an automatic process, you can set a goal for yourself: a business goal to never have a dirty pile of tent tops again, and that is key for your business.

HOW IT GOT DONE #1: Willy owns a smaller tent rental company in Maryland. He did not want to expand his building but needed to become more efficient. He bought a tent washer and installed it outside. Now he washes all of his tents a day before they go out and sets them up wet. He always has the cleanest tents in town and it took no extra space. As a bonus, Willy keeps his tops so clean throughout the year that he does not have to do winter washing or plan to make space for that purpose.

HOW IT GOT DONE #2: Richard runs the operations of Ace Party in Flushing, New York. Richard ran his numbers and determined that creating a mechanized way to wash his tents was a must. However, he was in Long Island, NY, and he literally could not buy another building to expand – they are not available in this area. Richard was forced to deal with the already too small space he had. To solve this, he created space through using time. Richard noticed that there was extra space in his building for about eight hours every day, so he built his cleaning operations around this space and they clean for eight hours every day. What was this space? It is the space that his trucks park in at night. During the day, they are out delivering and rarely all return at the same time throughout the day.

HOW IT GOT DONE #3: Carlos had a similar problem with space and he, too, used an element of time. Carlos owns Diamonette Party Rental in Miami, Florida. He was a growing company and could not justify the extra space he needed to hang dry his growing tent inventory. Carlos kept focusing on the isle ways between his shelving as a potential place to dry tents. The only problem was that he could only use this space at night to dry tents but he also occasionally needed to use some of the same space during the day when forklifts needed to travel down these isles.

So Carlos did something unique. He developed an automatic tent hanging system that allowed him to hang tents in every other isle of a less busy part of his building. Now, if a forklift operator wanted to use the isle where tents were hanging, all they had to do was press a button and the tents would travel on a track into the next isle over and the forklift operator was free to travel down the previously crowded isle. It was a great solution for Carlos' operation.

To learn more about this type of tent drying system, call Brian at 1-877-712-9172.

Chapter Five

How to Leverage Clean Tents to Increase Sales

Is it possible to eliminate customer complaints about dirty tent tops?

It absolutely is, yet I constantly hear from people that it's not. Most of these people's solutions are right in front of them. They simply haven't stopped, taken a moment to really study their business, and set a new goal to eliminate the complaints. And when they tell themselves that it's possible to do it and start looking for solutions to make that happen, that's when the real magic starts. They've got to accept that it can be done. And when it can be done, real profits start flowing into the business.

Why is it imperative to always have clean tops?

It's important to have clean tops because this is your biggest source for business referrals. When you put a clean top up, that customer tells others or people at that party call you later because you had clean tops. Having clean tops is great advertising; it reduces your advertising budget and saves you money.

It also encourages repeat customers because, when you have a clean product, they will most likely continue to buy from you automatically. It's been said that it costs three to five times more to go find a new customer than to have a repeat customer. So why not go ahead and spend a little extra time getting a clean top to encourage that repeat customer rather than spending three to five times more on your advertising budget to go out and find a new customer?

You can also demand higher prices by consistently having a premium product. So if you consistently have a clean top, you can consistently charge more, and when you consistently charge more, you have to understand that whether you're putting a dirty tent up or a clean tent, your costs are exactly the same. So if your costs are the same and you can charge more for a clean tent, it means you're putting more money in your pocket.

How does eliminating complaints contribute to your bottom line profits?

By eliminating your customer complaints, you no longer have to send crews out to replace a dirty tent top or go out on site to clean. If you do have to do that, it's a lost cost for you. And often it happens in your busiest time that you don't have crews available. So this means that you're going to be spending a lot of overtime cost sending a crew back out to get that tent top cleaned for the customer's satisfaction, and over time, it could be very, very costly, especially in the busy season when you don't have the manpower to do it or the manpower that you do have is already extremely tired.

What is the competitive edge to consistently having clean tops?

Consistency is key. If your competitor doesn't have a system to clean tops every time at the same level or quality as your business does, your business will grow. So if your competitor has consistently dirty tops and you consistently have clean tops, you will have the competitive edge. By building a system around cleaning tent tops when you know that your competitor doesn't, you're automatically going to get a growing business for yourself.

How will my stress level go down by having clean tent tops?

Well, if you have dirty tent tops, all it takes is one angry customer and, as an owner, you have that angry customer that calls you on the phone and it can ruin the rest of your day. It has a way of increasing stress when you have to deal with less than satisfied customers, no matter how much you think you can just push it aside.

You are the leader of the company as the owner or manager, and when you go on to your next interaction with your employees or with a customer, people pick up on the fact that you are worried or stressed. You're slightly different than you were prior to taking that customer complaint call. They tend to pick up on that; your employees will not want to follow you and they will not be excited about doing as good a job for you because you are not as nice to be around. People like to be around nice people.

So if you can eliminate angry customer calls coming in to you, you can become a better leader. You will become a better sales person and your customer satisfaction for all the people that you deal with will go way up. Basically, by having clean tops and not having angry customers calling, you will eliminate a source of frustration for yourself. And we know in this business that there are many other areas of frustration, so the more of those you can eliminate, the better off you are.

Chapter Six

Increase Your Income by 20% or More Without Doing Anything

How can clean tops improve your income by 20-30%?

You have to study your numbers. You have to understand your laundry volume. You have to understand what drains your profit and have specific numbers from dirty tent tops. And you have to reduce the owner and manager's stress.

Why is taking a break so hard for tent rental owners and managers?

When I talk about taking a break, I mean stop *doing* in your business. So often in this business, we love to put up tents and we're very good at our craft, so we're programmed to do and we're not programmed to stop and think; taking time to think often feels very awkward. But Peter Drucker said it best. He said, "What gets measured and tracked grows."

And it's important to understand what insanity is all about. Insanity is doing the same thing over and over again, expecting different results. If you don't know what activities in your business are most profitable for you, you might be doing the same wrong thing over and over again and not producing the profits that you need.

So it's important that you stop, take a break, and start thinking about what's most profitable for your business. You must stop doing, you must measure progress, you must look at your numbers, you must analyze, and you must study ways to have the most profitable plan to move forward. You must set goals.

Very often, as a person who started the business or manages the business, this is awkward. So, I would highly advise that you get help from others. If you're completely lost in this, there are plenty of advisors out there who can help you. Others could be your employees, your accountant, your lawyer, or other people who understand productivity, but get other people to help you!

Otherwise, if we don't stop and think, we don't know what we don't know and we'll consistently think that we're growing the business while we're actually doing all the wrong things and, as a result, not growing nearly as productively or as profitably as we potentially could.

Do you know what in your company is draining your profits?

This is really important to understand because it's a key area in business that people forget. They forget a very fundamental accounting principle: profit – or money in your pocket – equals your revenue or your sales, minus your expenses. And it's important to continually go back to that so that you can understand what is draining your profit.

In the tent rental business, our revenue is our sales. So when you go set a tent up for a customer, the price is set. You already know before the trucks take off what that price is going to be. But the next step is absolutely key. The expenses – the money out of your pocket – varies wildly in our industry. If the wind's blowing that day, if it's too hot, if it's too cold, if you have too hard a surface to drive a tent stake in, or dirty tent tops that you have to stop and clean at any level on the way, those expenses tend to go up.

And when those expenses that vary so wildly go up and your revenue is set already, guess what? It's actually taking money out of your pocket. As the owner or manager, it's taking money or income out of your pocket because that's the profit that's left. You need to control these expenses, and if you control these expenses, you will have more money in your pocket. You need to stop, study, and analyze. When you do that, you'll find what drains money out of your business, and once you understand what that is, you can set goals and build plans to remedy these drains.

How do dirty tent tops affect an owner's income?

Key factors: labor and overtime cost, cost disruption in the business, and busy times. So when you're really busy and some of these varied costs come around, it slows things down and causes disruptions in the business.

When you don't have enough A-grade tops to satisfy the number of high-profit jobs you can get, you are in essence hurting your profitability and business potential. So having more A-grade tops means you can get more money in the door while having the same expenses going out.

Negative customer referrals, spending more time on marketing and advertising; this just increases your sales cost and decreases your profit. So, by having clean tents, you get customer positive referrals and you can actually spend less money on marketing and advertising. By having a surefire way to have clean tents, you will eliminate low employee morale around the task of washing and decrease your management cost because you won't have low morale employees and you will have less employee turnover. So you can have employees that actually like doing the work and will do a good job for you and stay with you longer.

Having a system to keep tent tops clean affects all areas of your business and can bring you big profits.

How do I reduce stress and grow a tent rental company?

You've got to build systems. Start studying your numbers and setting goals, and start measuring and tracking those goals. And when you have systems around your business, it means when you get busy that's one less frustration you have. That system also means that the employees who are involved in it know how to do a good job, know what's expected of them, and they can actually achieve the goals that you set for them.

TIP – *Read the book The E-Myth Revisited by Michael E. Gerber. It is the book that changed my business life. It forced me to look at tent rental in a totally different way. You can get a copy at* www.teecosoltuions.com/emyth.

You can reduce your stress and grow a tent rental company by gaining control and eliminating chaos. You'll ensure that everything your company is doing is the right thing for the most profitable growth. You'll enjoy the business again and everyone around you will start to see and feel this about you, and as a result, they will want to jump on your bandwagon and help you.

Steve Arendt

Chapter Seven

Four Secrets to Staying on Track During Your Busiest Times

How do I keep up in busy times?

To keep up in busy times, there are four key secrets:

- Plan ahead.
- Effectively use your space.
- Make sure that you have systems set up.
- Have an emergency plan in place.

How can planning ahead help me keep up with dirty tents in busy times?

It's best to set a goal, and the best goal is to eliminate the dirty pile; especially in your busy time. The effect of that goal on your business during the busy time is phenomenal. Your business will be much more effective and allow for the best use of your inventory. The technical term for the goal I'm talking about is "shelf-ready in 24 hours."

If a tent top comes back dirty, no matter what the situation or how busy you are, you should have a goal to get it back on the shelf, clean, within 24 hours, or at least ready to be re-rented within 24 hours.

TIP: *To make this happen, make somebody accountable for it. Put somebody in charge. This person can improve your inventory management. This person's job is to know what tops are coming in and what kind of condition they will be in. Most of the time, you can know that well before they actually come in. A tent top that went out clean on Friday while the weather was nice all day and was taken down in the middle of the afternoon on the following Monday after the dew dried is most likely going to come back clean. That person, if they're paying attention, should know that the odds are this tent is going to be clean when it comes back.*

The converse is true, too; if that tent went out, it rained all weekend, and the ground was saturated when they had to take it down, it's probably going to come back dirty because they dropped it in the mud just to get it down and back to the shop. So the inventory manager, the person who's accountable for that, should know.

For the goal of eliminating the dirty pile, that person should be able to plan ahead and make provisions to get that tent top clean in 24 hours and ready to go back out.

How can I keep up in my current space and do it with the same labor cost I currently have?

Add a second shift. Keep in mind that, in your busy time, trying to use the same people to install the tents and to clean your tents can cause problems. In your busy time, you're very often getting tired. It's what I call the 15-day wall. After 14 days, the wheels tend to fall off of your company. It's 14 days of working really hard in a busy time when people get tired, the morale goes down, and inefficiencies become common.

On the 15th day, very simple mistakes start happening that affect the whole company. They affect relationships with customers; they affect the relationship in a psychological sense, they affect the quality that you're giving the customer, and they affect the way internal systems operate, resulting in what end up being very costly mistakes. This is a key concept to understand.

If you're adding a second shift, it only takes two or three people. You can actually use the space that is not available to you during the busy time of the day. So by having your second shift come in after your installation crews have left, and after the people who are in the warehouse have left, it allows you to use the space that you normally couldn't use during the busy part of the day.

You're also going to reduce your overtime by not asking that same crew of people who are your installers and regular warehouse people to do the washing, so they are no longer kicked into overtime pay. The people who are coming on your second shift are starting at regular pay.

It also does another very important thing because it keeps your installers fresh. You're keeping their work hours down, allowing them to go home and disconnect from the business and get their mind and body rested so that when they come back the next day, they're fresh and can do a better job installing tents and dealing with customers (because they're not spending the evening washing tents).

And the next morning, if you didn't have a system in place, you would have to scramble through a dirty pile to get the cleanest of the dirty tents back on the truck and set up, having a negative impact on the *customer* in terms of putting up a dirty tent.

How can I possibly keep up with the volume of dirty tent tops in my busy time?

You have to develop written systems and procedures. You, as the owner or manager, may understand clearly how to keep up in your busy times, but you have to develop a system or procedure that's written down so that everyone else, including the newest employees, can understand how that's supposed to happen in your business. Without it being written down, you don't have a system and you don't have procedures. So you have to develop these types of systems and procedures to have even the possibility of keeping up during your busy times.

I would highly advise you to develop these systems and procedures when things are slow; when you have time to think, when you have time to get the help of employees who actually understand what it means to be busy. I would invite you to get these employees to sit around the table and spell out what you're trying to do so you can develop systems and procedures that are going to work within the confines of the existing space that you have. The goal would be to get the tent tops that come back dirty (no matter how busy you are or what kind of volume you have) cleaned within 24 hours and ready to go back out.

Let them help you with the solution. Be very open-minded, throw everything on the table, and be collaborative. You'll be amazed at what happens when you're able to enlist the help and insights of your employees. These are the people who do it every day. You, as a manager or owner, don't do it every day. Leverage what they know and see.

It will also empower them; it will make them better employees and they'll have a higher level of buy-in for the systems and procedures that are developed, and they will actually follow it a lot more willingly than if it just came from the owner or the manager.

In developing systems and procedures, I would also highly recommend that you see other operations. If you have a good relationship with your competitor, go there. Many people don't have that good relationship, but the party rental industry is generally extremely open. Get outside of your competitive range geography-wise and make a call to somebody who operates out of a similar a space as you, has a similar volume of tents, and see how they do it. They may not have the complete answer, but at least you could pick up a tidbit here or there. That can add to developing your system a little bit further.

And see multiple operations. Take some time and make a road trip out of it! If you don't know who to go see, tap into your vendors. These vendors have seen multiple people in their travels in the course of the year, they have relationships out there, and they're willing to leverage for you. Ask them a favor to make an introduction; they would be more than happy to do it.

Go to trade shows like the MATRA show, the ARA show, and the IFAI show and network with others; start talking. You'll also find out that they'd be more than willing to open up and have you visit their operation. So reach out to other operators across the country who may have similar situations as you. You're not alone in this and the problems you're trying to solve.

And lastly, when talking about developing systems and procedures, you have to make it teachable and repeatable. You may have developed a great system and a great procedure, but you have to think about the new employee coming in. If it's the middle of your busy season and you have to hire a new employee, the first day or the first week that the employee shows up, you have to think about it. Are you allowing that employee to be the best employee that they can? The very first step is the on-boarding step that includes training from your written systems manual. This allows that employee to become the best employee that they can.

In the on-boarding process, are you teaching in the system of cleaning that you've developed so that they can actually do it the way that you planned? And if it's not you teaching that person, who's in charge of teaching that person and what resources do they have to ensure that the employee fully understands the systems and procedures the way you had envisioned them as the creator? Very, very important: make it teachable and repeatable so the on-boarding of any employee coming into your business is a lot easier. You'll experience a much better rate of success that way.

What about the times when everything comes back dirty? How do I deal with this?

Here's your answer: have a backup plan for emergencies. The most common emergency that I get feedback from is a rainy weekend. When most of the tents are going out during a busy season and it rains over the weekend, it's the dread. Very often I get reports back from rental companies that talk about how they can never catch up to the rest of their tent rental season because of one weekend when most of their inventory was out and it actually rained. This is an exemplary case of an emergency time where a backup plan for emergencies would be very, very valuable.

We talked about having an inventory manager earlier and they should know when it's coming back four to five days in advance. They have access to the weather reports and how many tents are coming back on a particular day. They should be able to forecast with great accuracy what type of tents are coming back, when they're coming back, how dirty they might be, and from there be able to have a good handful of days as a cushion to execute an emergency backup plan.

So, what does an emergency backup plan look like? What are some of the elements? You might want to understand how you can use the space outside of your building to wash if you have to. You might want to find buildings that you can use temporarily. Reach out to your friends who may own businesses, reach out to the businesses that are in the same complex as you are, reach out to your landlord who may have extra buildings that you could use on a temporary basis. Get extremely creative as far as where you can find buildings that you can use temporarily for a handful of days.

Also, think about contract washing; form relationships. If you know a handful of days in advance that you're going to have a bunch of dirty tents coming back, are you willing to put them in a truck and drive them up to 100 miles away and wait for them to be washed? Maybe they'll come back wet, but you can send them back out wet. But have a relationship with a contract washer who can wash them at a much quicker pace than you can. If you give them enough advance notice, they can set up a second or third shift and get your stuff done perhaps in the middle of the night. Contract washing is a great way to set up a backup plan.

Another easy way to set up a backup plan is to have a system to work a second and third shift. You can access people for this on a temporary basis. Access firemen – volunteer firemen or firemen who tend to have work four to five days straight and then have seven or eight days off. These are great people to get for temporary work. How about friends of the college kid you have working for you? They have friends that are often available on short notice and they can rearrange their schedules.

And think about other pockets that are unique to your area that you might be able to tap into. Very often it's retired people who are just looking for something to do. Systems that involve second or third shifts in your building use a space that normally can't be used during the busy time and tap into temporary labor pools that are unique to the area that you're in.

TIP – I have seen a handful of clients faced with dealing with huge volumes of wet tents that they could not get dried quickly enough in their busy times. Wet tents stored for even short periods can be cause for mold growth and this compounds the problems of dealing with an already busy business. One customer rented refrigerated tractor trailers and kept the wet tents cold enough so the mold could not grow. Another had access to local warehouse space that was refrigerated (think about space that stores produce); he rented space in this warehouse and stored his wet tents until he could deal with them properly.

Steve Arendt

Chapter Eight

Drying Doesn't Have to Hold You Back – Learning to be Different

What are some tips for drying?

There are various methods for drying the tents. Obviously, the downfall of not having a dry tent is folding it up wet and, even though it's clean, it will get mildew or mold in it. Unfortunately, when you go to put that tent back up, the white tent that you folded up is now black because of the mold.

It's very important to understand that, in every geographic region of the world, mold will develop at different rates. Typically, if it's a little bit colder like up in the northern regions of the northern hemisphere, the rates of mold tend to be less. So you can fold the tent up wet in a colder atmosphere and it won't tend to get moldy as quickly as it would in a warmer, moist atmosphere. This is why we want to have it dry; we want to avoid mold.

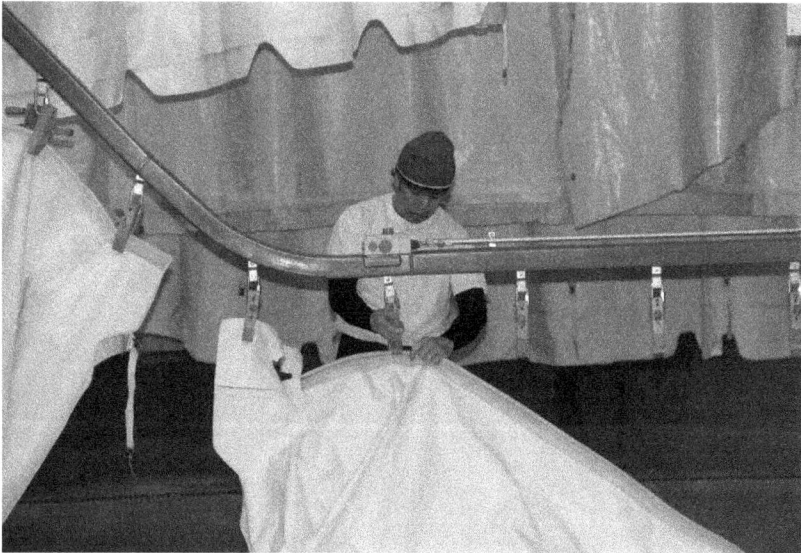

Probably the most common way to dry tents is with a block and tackle system or a pulley system from the ceiling. So you have ropes and pulleys up in the ceiling where you can tie the end of the rope onto a particular piece of the tent and then pull that up, and tie the other end of the rope off to a concrete weight, an anchor, a shelving unit, or whatever and allow that tent to hang, just like in the days when your grandmother hung her clothes outside.

You have to be careful about using this method for a couple of different reasons. You have to make sure that the people tying the ropes to the tent know how to tie them in such a way that they're not attached to weaker parts of the tent that will rip as soon as they lift the tent up. So they have to understand how to tie it in such a way that it doesn't destroy the tent.

You also have to be careful when you put pulleys up in the ceiling not to exceed snow loads or excess loads that weather might put on the ceiling. Ceilings and roofs are often rated for snow, and if you have all of your tents hung up and snow comes along, you have too much weight for that ceiling and risk a failure. So it's not just as easy sometimes as tying pulleys up into the rafters of our ceiling; you really have to be cognizant of those extenuating circumstances.

You also have to be very strategic about where you put those pulleys and what kind of space you take up in your building. You have to pay attention to your daily workflow. So, if you hang tent tops in the morning and they're in the way of your daily workflow of getting trucks loaded or inventory off or back on the shelf, you are creating cost in the business very unintentionally through the wrong strategic placement of those tent tops.

You can do various strategic things like hanging them in the evening after all the other work is done, taking up that space that's not going to be used during the evening. You can also be very strategic in how you actually get the drying done.

How much space you are going to have between each tent that you hang (where you tie your pulleys up on the ceiling) is key. If you want to hang them very close together to conserve space, you're going to have to think a lot about what kind of air flow goes between those tents, because if you don't have any air flow between them, your drying times are going to be very slow.

A very common goal that I would set forth if I were limited on my space would be to go ahead and hang those tents fairly close together. Another goal would be to have them dry by the next morning, so you could send a crew in an hour or two early to drop those tents and get them folded and back on the shelf, or at least ready to go back out so that when the normal crew shows up, those tents are not in their way for their daily workflow of the usual business operations.

But if you hang them very close to each other, you have to be very conscious that you need to get air flowing all night long at a decent rate between those tents. That might mean putting ceiling fans up. You may also have to put fans below that blow air into the sides of those tents while making sure that air flows all the way throughout the building, including in the middle of all those tents; that's a sure way to get them dry. So those are some of the things that you want to think about when you're hanging with block and tackle.

You also want to think about the quality of the air. Really moist air tends to dry tents very slowly. Mother Nature often provides free, dry air that is outside of your building; it is much drier than the inside, so you may want to think about adding some exhaust fans so that when the tents start to dry and all that moisture ends up in the air inside the building, you can actually push it outside. If the air outside is drier than what you have inside, drag that drier air in and help the rate at which these tent tops get dry. After all, it's the rate of drying that's key for your business.

In some climates, you could move to a different style of drying. You can actually hang them outside. I've seen people put telephone poles up, I've seen them tied to their buildings; hang them outside much like you would hang inside with a block and tackle system. You must be aware of the dust and rain, though. If you hang it up and the rain is coming that evening, it's going to carry with it some dust. It's going to drag all the dust out of the air and put it right back on your tent top.

If you're in a dusty environment, even though it's not raining and the sun's out, if the wind tends to blow it will blow that dust right up on your tent. It's critical that you be aware that this might happen when hanging outside, so pay attention to that. Otherwise, hanging outside can be a very great way to utilize your space and get some drying done in a quick fashion because you get to use the wind and the sun.

Another effective way to dry tents is to actually get them washed and send them out wet. It doesn't work for every company; I often see it working very well for small to medium size companies. I also see it working very well for 40-foot wide tents and below, so the smaller tents. It works well for keder-style tents, too.

When you go to install a wet tent, you can almost immediately drag it over some sort of frame and minimize the time it touches the ground, thus reducing the opportunity for the top to pick up dirt. Note that it doesn't work so well for a pole tent unless you spend a fair amount of time putting some clean ground cloths out before you drag that tent out wet and spread it on the drop cloths to set it up.

Sending tent tops out wet allows you to go ahead and just wash them and fold them up. In the worse climates, you've got a good 20 to 24 hours before the mold is going to start. That would probably be the worst case scenario you might see in a warm, moist climate where mold is a problem. But most of the time, you're going to have 24 to 36 hours before mold starts, so you can fold them up wet, get them to the job site, and get them set up. If you look at the inventory of a small to medium size company, very often that's the majority of their inventory. So, addressing the busy time with the potential of just sending the tent out wet is key.

Very often the kickback I get on this idea is that it's going to take more time in the field to put the wet tent up. And indeed, it will, that's a great observation. But if you compare that to the amount of time it would take you to deal with getting it dry back in a space that's typically smaller – for a small to medium size company especially – hanging it up, making sure that it's dry, dropping it back down, folding it up, putting it back on the truck... that amount of time is often more than the amount of extra time you have to deal with it in the field because it's wet. In the end, when you compare the two, the lesser of two evils is just dealing with it wet in the field.

I also challenge people in this area to develop systems and procedures that are clear for everybody in the field as far as how to deal with wet tent tops. How do they get folded? What kind of drop cloths do you use? How do you pull them over the frames? And so forth. So developing a system and procedure that's clear for everybody in the field when dealing with wet tent tops is important. Once they're up, Mother Nature can take it from there.

The other way to deal with getting tents dry is to use drying machines. It's very important to understand that a regular commercial linen dryer can be detrimental to a tent. Clothes or fabric sheets – any type of woven fabric – can often handle much more heat than a PVC-based product. What you end up doing when you put a PVC-based product into a commercial drying machine is melt the PVC or the vinyl. Even if it's not visible, it will happen on a microscopic level.

When using a commercial dryer, you also very often end up shrinking any type of webbing, so I have seen framed tent tops that can't be stretched over their frames because the webbing got shrunk in the drying process.

So when you're using drying machines, you have to be very conscious of a couple of factors. The first one is obviously the temperature; you have to use lower temperatures. You also have to be focused on the fact that you're drying a very large piece of material. Getting the air to go into the middle of the material where the folds and the wetness are is often a challenge in a commercial drying machine because the fabric that you're drying doesn't allow air to go through it, unlike shirts, sheets, or linen table cloths.

So the middle part of the wad of tents in that machine is harder to get dry in a commercial machine. If you're going to use a dryer, you want to pay special attention to the volume of the drum so that the middle of that tent can come apart and be exposed to the air that's blowing over it. So dryers are a viable option, but you have to pay very close attention to the design of the dryer so it dries safely and effectively.

The last drying system is a trolley system. A trolley system is very unique. This is a great way to use invisible space not normally accessible. You can hook a tent top to a trolley and send it to spaces in your buildings where you normally can't use a ladder to even get up into the higher areas, for instance behind some shelving. If you take your shelving unit and move it out about 10 inches, you can install the trolley system up in the ceiling and allow that tent to be hooked up in the normal drying area and then sent behind that shelving unit to be dried. It's a space of 10 inches that you're probably not going to miss, but it allows that tent top to be hung and has space around it to dry. You might be able to send it behind shelving units that are hundreds of feet long.

You can also circle that trolley system around and come back behind other shelving units or between shelving units if you just spread them apart a few inches. It's a great way to utilize space that you normally wouldn't have access to and couldn't even use to hang your tents.

Trolley systems are an awesome way to do it. A little more capital intensive, but less than the expense of expanding a building.

Steve Arendt

Chapter Nine

Conclusion

Technically, keeping party tent tops clean is not much different that washing dishes at home. A dirty plate can be washed in cold water with no dish soap and wiped with a hand. Perhaps this is a great method if one is camping in the woods. But for those interested in a slightly easier way, adding a bit of warm water, dish soap, and letting the plate soak for a moment is a much easier way to clean dishes. For a family or larger group, there is an even better way: buy a dish washing machine. Even buying a dish washing machine requires some study. Do you buy one that washes for a commercial setting, one that washes fast, one that washes small loads, one that conserves water... many options are available. Washing dishes is easy, but a person camping in the woods has an entirely different solution than a person who is washing for a large family or restaurant.

Keeping tent tops clean is really no different. A simple hand washing operation that uses mops, brushes, and some cleaning agent is a great solution for a small company or a company that is just getting started. Perhaps the only questions a startup company has to answer is what type of brush, mop, or rag will they use and what is the best chemical to use. Yet, as the company grows and the volume of laundry grows, other questions demand answers. Questions like where is the best space to do the washing? Who are the best people to do the washing? Where do we find these people? How much laundry can we get done in a work shift? Can we keep up?

By now you may realize that your company is unique and coming up with the perfect tent cleaning solution for your situation requires you to stop and think. It requires you to understand the level of clean you must maintain for your business. It requires that you develop systems to keep up in busy times. It requires you to learn how to best utilize your inventory. It requires you to find solutions to all these questions and execute your plan with the space and manpower that is available to you.

We can easily teach you how to get certain stains out or how to wash a tent. But if you only get one thing from this book, get this:

Tent tops that sit in dirty piles or on shelves do not make you money! The only tent tops that make you money are the clean ones set up at a customer's site.

Learning how to wash a tent is just the first step! Learning how to eliminate your dirty piles and keep more tents set up at your customers' sites is where you will make most of your money and reduce most of your stress.

If you are ready to take the next step to reduce stress and make more money, we can help. Call us at 1-877-712-9172 to set up a meeting with one of our team. Or you can go to www.TeecoConsult.com right now and have access to a team member's calendar to set up your appointment.

Demand the cleanest tents in town with...

Free resources available to you - now!

Are you ready to eliminate your dirty pile of tents... FOREVER? Are you ready to take all the powerful business-building ideas you learned in this book and put them to work in your business?

Then the team at Teeco Solutions wants to help you.
Visit: www.TeecoSolutions.com
where you will find:

- Your free DVD course on how to test for the right cleaning chemicals
- Special deals on cleaning chemicals
- Access to free reports on better business practices for your tent rental company
- Information about whether a tent washing machine or dryer is right for your business
- Peer input about eliminating the worry of ever having a customer call about a dirty tent top
- And More!

Find out what the most successful small and large tent rental companies already know. Visit:

www.TeecoSolutions.com

www.ingramcontent.com/pod-product-compliance
Lightning Source LLC
Chambersburg PA
CBHW050619210326
41521CB00008B/1319